lay pastorate

reg legg

lay pastorate

reg legg

Acknowledgements

The quotation on p.12 is taken from *The Foolishness of God* by John Austin Baker published and copyright 1970 by Darton Longman & Todd Ltd., and is used by permission of the publishers.

The quotation on p.11 is taken from *God's Kingdom and Ours* by Fr Hebert, published and copyright by SCM Press, and is used by permission of the publishers.

The quotation on p.11 is taken from *The Faith of the People of God* by John Macquarrie, published and copyright by SCM Press and is used by permission of the publishers.

The quotation on p.20 is taken from *Theology and Joy* by Jurgen Moltmann, published and copyright 1973 by SCM Press, and is used by permission of the publisher.

The quotation on p.12 is taken from *Priest or President* by A.E. Harvey, published by SPCK 1975, and is used by permission of the publishers.

First Published in 1989 by Angel Press
P.O. Box 60, East Wittering, West Sussex PO20 8RA

British Library Cataloguing in Publication Data

Legg, Reg
Lay pastorate.
1. Church of England. Role of Laity
I. Title
262'.15

ISBN 0 – 947785 – 29 – 9

Typeset in Bodoni by Woodfield Graphics, Fontwell, Sussex.
Printed in Great Britain by Hollen Street Press, Slough, Berks.

Contents

Everything depends
on the end from which
you are looking at it......

ONE

The Animals At The Zoo

Everything depends on the end from which you are looking at it, as the man said before getting hooked up with the rhinoceros. Indeed, the whole emotional overtones of a subject depend on the end from which you look at it. Doubtless the chap viewing the rhinoceros from the blunt end at the time could possibly see something at least a little humorous in the sight – and be forgiven for doing so provided that he did not know that Fred was up at the sharp end.

The problem now arises: 'How do you describe a rhino?' The blunt-ender says 'Funny'. The sharp-ender says, 'Terrifying' (assuming he still wants to talk). But you and I being wise people – and not involved in the situation with quite so much immediacy – know very well that there is also the side view of the rhinoceros to be had, and that it is not, for most of its time, charging around looking funny or terrifying. From the beam, we have to add words like 'curious', 'awesome', 'prehistoric', 'majestic'. . . even 'gentle'. Let's say that Job could just as well have meant the rhino as the crocodile by 'behemoth'.

What strength is in his loins!
what power in the muscles of his belly!. . .
Can you fill his skin with harpoons?. . .
Who has ever undone his outer garment
or penetrated his doublet of hide?
Sword or spear, dagger or javelin,
if they touch him they have no effect. . .

Oh, what a poem!

And that's what happens when one sees a creature not as a funny end or a sharp end but as a whole – the poetry gets in and gives a bit of room for wonder.

We are in a perpetual problem about talking-about-things – or, more particularly, a problem in talking of 'things-as-they-are'; when we want to convey something, it seems that we must necessarily talk about its 'bits'. . . and one can think of nothing less rainbow-like than describing a rainbow as 'white light split into its constituent colours'! – nothing less rhino-like than 'a quadruped with a horn on its nose and its eyes in the wrong place living in a skin a few sizes too large'. Would that we could leave it all to the poet!

But, sadly, we cannot. Especially when it comes to God-talk. Here more than anywhere we are stuck with the language of 'sharp end' and 'blunt end'. Once say 'God', and you have to think of a Being 'greater than that which can be thought': transcendent. Yet one has to think of Him also as immersed in, involved with 'all that can be thought: immanent. Try to get a view from the side, and you end up saying 'God' again. . . just about as useful as saying a rhinoceros is a rhinoceros. And the difficulty filters through the whole Christian vocabulary. Say 'church' and you must write an essay about what you mean before you can go on – the building, the congregation, the whole People of God, or even just 'parsons'. The bits have taken over the whole! The rhino is his skin!?

It is to the whole People of God that we must turn now.

Immediately there springs to mind a memory of being instituted in a parish where, for the occasion, a well-meaning Sunday School teacher had given her charges their heads to do their thing: the porch was overwhelmed with poster-paint and a lot of cotton-wool proclaiming, 'The Vicar is the shepherd and we are the sheep.'Protest was of no avail. They were determinedly sheepish – and the bulk of them very thick-coated and well-heeled sheep too. But most parsons will have experienced the next thing; the discovery that one has inherited the only surviving breed of Sabre-toothed Sheep! (Canterbury Sheep if you are in the southern English province.) There can be few who have not heard the great Christian cry: 'We'll soon have him used to our ways!'

In fairness one must equally recall the picture of the parson who arrives with missionary zeal, light of battle and all – and a fairish big Sword of the Spirit which sharpens sheep's brains remarkably and sends them in all directions as, determined on the Conversion of Britain in this generation if not sooner, he pursues them with the battle-cry: 'By God, they shall conform or I will harry them from the land!' Six of one and half-dozen of the other, then. But where is the People of God? The story of The Church of England is littered with anti-clerical laity and lay-despising clerics, joining only in a hatred of anything labelled 'theologian'. Of course, these are black and white pictures. . . cartoons. Their existence just like that is rare. But, given some pastelling in patches, they are not unrecognisable; and the sad thing is that, behind these cartoons, there is a lot of very destructive double-think going on.

Take the Sheep, for instance. There are some straightforward ones who look to be led to their pasture – but not many. Most, one may suspect, are – albeit subconsciously – abdicating. They are being sheepish to get out of their own real task. . . which is to be Shepherds. They are abdicating their own duty to minister by manoeuvring the poor old Revd Bloggs into a position where he has to feel that it is his solo job to do all the ministering. He's paid for it. They, the sheep will suggest, are there to 'back him up' and to meet the cost of his ministering. . . provided it stays within reason.

Now Revd Bloggs may react in one of two ways. He may be one of these poor chaps with an overpowering sense of duty who thinks that the sheep are genuine, in which case he takes an increasing load of the world's cares on his shoulders and either drops some and picks up a load of guilt instead. Or he may be the kind of chap who gets a sort of martyred satisfaction out of the game, fills his waking hours with rush and busy, and then gets to feeling guilty because he 'never seems to have time to spend with folk'. But even worse is possible! He may turn into St. Athanasius Bloggs, modern version: a top-flight management man, aware that his sheep have set him on a pedestal and rather enjoying the view from the pedestal. . . even the view of himself! He ends up by talking about 'my parish' and 'my people'. Meanwhile, down on the farm, the crafty lot of sheep are having a smashing time, with their call to ministry reduced to a Very Low Common Denominator: Fred's in hospital? Tell the Vicar. Joe and Sarah's marriage is busting at the seams? Tell the Vicar. Old Gert can't afford to keep her fire alight? Tell the Vicar. What a marvellous, holy-sounding get-out! We may be 'Christian men and women, always willing, never able'. . . but we told the Vicar!

Next move.

Revd Bloggs, or Father Bloggs, or St. A-Bloggs (if he hasn't had a breakdown) develops a system to cope. If, that is, he doesn't get round to telling the Church what it should be doing. Having his system, he now turns it into his job specification. Bad enough. . . but he also begins to see the People of God as a rather useless lot of hangers-on to the Church. He becomes clericalised and develops a slight sense of contempt for the Laity. Here is another smirk-making memory: being told by an elderly parson, 'You must remember these people (his congregation!) are theological babies.' The congregation in question was made up of loads of lads and lasses with enough honours degrees in such a vast variety of subjects that they could have staffed a university!

But you see where we have arrived. There are the clergy, resentfully or willingly, made into the horn of the rhinoceros. And there are the laity, the backside of the beast, existing just to push the horn along up front!

Whatever became of the rhino?!

You may care to stop at this point and ask whether the cartoons here are even *slightly* suggesting some of your own attitudes – as individual, as a congregation of the People of God, as parson, as layman?

And perhaps spend a moment with Ephesians 5:1-2.

Can you see that as 'Tell the Vicar'?

What, then, is your 'offering'?

Can it be worked out solely in terms of prayer/worship?

TWO

The Zoo Itself or Up the Institution

Or even 'Three cheers for the job-specification!' Let's all have our tasks defined. Then we can say to God: 'I have done all I ought to do. Set my throne at your right hand in the Kingdom.' And either 'I ruled my sheep with a crook that never let 'em wander', or 'I told the Vicar' – according to whether you are clergy or laity.

Somehow, it doesn't seem likely God will buy it.

And you notice we had to put in that either/or.

Once we get God-talk down to Church-talk – should one say 'down'? Ought Church-talk not to be the same as God-talk? Once we get God-talk turning into Church-talk, we are stuck with horn and rear – stuck with an inhibiting clergy/laity thing. But the *laos* – the laity – is the People of God. The sense came straight out of Old Israel; direct from Egypt, through Hosea and into Romans 9:24. No sign of clergy or laity. The whole lot are God's *laos*. Yet what a sad thing it is to see in the Oxford Dictionary of the Christian Church: 'LAITY. Members of the Christian Churches who do not belong to the clergy'! The People of God are just not-things! Nothing positive about 'em at all. Wrong way round, surely. Let's try again, starting with

'CLERGY': 'Members of the People of God who are called to a particular sacramental role within the People.' But, of course, we can no longer use the word *laos* as it was meant to be; for too long it has had the wrong meaning: 'LAYMAN: slightly shop-soiled, sub-standard churchgoer!'

'People of God', then? But the biblical scholars will get it muddled with good old Israel. 'Body of Christ'? – But the sacramental reference will leave possibilities of misunderstanding. 'The Church' – Yes, of course it should be, but the institution has killed the word.

And there we have hit the bull: 'The institution'.

Strange how institutionalised churches have become, isn't it? There was this Jesus of Nazareth who spent his time telling the Jews that they had got bogged down in The Institution, and, institutionalists being what they are, they fixed him up with Mafia-like tactics. His followers managed for a while, and then. . . Pop! – and there was an institution. You can see it start with just about the most un-Christlike words in the New Testament, Acts 6:2. 'It would be a grave mistake for us to neglect the word of God in order to wait at table!' Can you imagine the Feet-Washer saying that? But they did. And they created the split-rhino. . . preachers and 'also-rans'. They had turned 'The Way' into an institution.

Now it is a fairly natural extension of Parkinson's Law to observe that institutions tend to multiply the number of people they need to prop up the institution far faster than they increase the number of people needed to fulfil the institution's objectives.

They also naturally create hierarchies which produce a situation whereby those at the top of the pyramid are led to feel that they carry the whole weight of responsibility for decision, while those at ground level feel (and possibly

rejoice in the fact) that they are absolved from any sort of initiative. So our Church (institutional rather than militant) splits clergy – especially bishops – off as those who are meant to call the shots, and the laity off as pew-fodder. An attempt to superimpose on the institution some sort of 'Lay Voice' reduces the situation to a worse confusion in which the laity feels it has a calling to 'keep an eye on the clergy and see what they get up to', while the clergy regard the laity as a batch of ignoramuses who don't know Mark from Malachi.

Whatever happened to the rhino's brains and innards?

***

I am aware that I have cartooned even more drastically here – SO – Would you like – preferably at a deeper level than an 'indignation meeting' – to re-write, add to, or subtract from my definition of the Clergy as 'Members of the People of God who are called to a particular sacramental role within the People.'

How does your ultimate definition square with what you see priests and ministers doing with their time?

Can you identify that which is laid upon you purely because of the institution? This is fairly easy to test. Ask, 'Can I imagine Jesus or Paul telling me to do it?'

And now you have arrived at the crunch question which may not finally be avoided. Is the institution as it is now shaped adequate for the task for which it was created?

***

After such unsettling and disquieting thoughts we had better seek some wisdom from our elders and betters. . .

THREE

The Wisdom of the Elephants

Nature's great masterpiece, an elephant.
The only harmless great thing.

John Donne

Within the Church-Zoo we must probably put our theologians as the elephants, for they are ever giving rides to the public, and are probably the only animals ranging

around the cages who are tall enough to see what is going on in them.

In the light of that, it is rather sad that the Church so often uses 'theologian' as a dirty word and, indeed, the attitude is rather incongruous inasmuch as anyone who says, 'God' and adds just one other word to it is, in fact, setting himself up as a theologian. Even to pray 'Lord, have mercy' is to say something about God: to 'do theology'.

So it is important to listen to the elephants.

During the latter half of the twentieth century, they have been saying quite a lot about what goes on in the cages – especially about this minister/people, clergy/laity thing.

'The evil of clericalism is that it violates the true principles of Church Order, since it prevents the laity from taking their proper share in the Church's life.' So wrote Fr. Hebert in 1959, and by 'clericalism' he meant precisely the game of setting up the clergyman as Big White Chief. He could equally have written 'seems to excuse' for 'prevents'! He goes on to note 'the general failure of the Church of England. . . to express in practice the share which all Christians have by rights in the common life of the Body of Christ' (*God's Kingdom and Ours*, SCM Press).

Thirteen years later, Professor Macquarrie, writing *The Faith of the People of God* (SCM Press) says, 'Christian ministry belongs in the first instance to the whole people of God. . . ministers themselves belong to the people of God.' 'The all-important ministry of the whole people can be exercised with full effect only when it gathers up in a harmonious unity the widest possible range of differing ministries.' 'We must not think of an ordained ministry and a lay ministry going on side by side. They belong together in the total ministry of the people, and must be in constant interaction.' 'Christian ministry is most effectively done not by individuals but by teams, and teams which include both lay and clerical members. . . the basic theological principles governing this situation are – collegiality, concelebration and, not least, co-theologizing.'

And the reaction of the zoo-cages to this thinking?

To go madly for more designated Lay Workers (full-time paid, of course. And, of course it was something you could let women do! Cor!).

The big, *big* problem – especially for the wool-died clergy – was that word 'concelebration'. Even the saintly John Austin Baker started rattling the cage – and the cage at Westminster Abbey at that! In *The Foolishness of God* (Darton, Longman and Todd) he wrote:

> One obvious step for the Christian Community is to draw part of its leadership now from the heads of the local secular community and to operate not only in the gathered congregations but also in the social groupings of the world. . . and this means not simply a seat on church councils but the right to perform certain offices, such as presiding at the Eucharist and teaching, which are at present confined to 'professional' ministers.

Now we are treading on the job-description toes!

The position was re-stated by A.E.Harvey in 1975. In *Priest or President* (SPCK) he writes:

> There seems no reason why order should seem to be threatened if the presidency has occasionally to be assumed by someone else – particularly if that person has been regularly prepared for such an emergency and has taken the minister's place by general consent and with due authorization.

***

No doubt the elephants were moving a bit far a bit fast: and actually seeing what was outside the walls of the zoo was too much for those who had not yet got outside their cages. Those other taller animals, the giraffes with the gently episcopal eyes, saw what the elephants saw; but since they were never let outside their cages, they understood something of what it all seemed like in the other cages and therefore counselled slow movement. The monkeys, of course, seized on this as counsel for doing nothing at all.

One reaches the point, here, where the question must be asked: 'What is the zoo for?' Presumably not for the animals to stare at one another and say, 'You do not have a reticulated hide, therefore you are not an animal,' or 'You have no decent horns therefore you are not an animal.'

But you do get quite a bit of that in the Christian Zoo!

No – the zoo exists for those other than the animals. Indeed it may prove to have purpose for the animals eventually, in preserving the vast range of peculiarity in their purpose and function in the total world-ecology; but in the first instance it exists to provoke the curiosity and wonder-at-the-universe of those outside the zoo, and secondly it exists to provide those whose curiosity has been aroused with the opportunities of deepening their understandings of that universe.

The Church is not other! It exists to proclaim to the world that the world has purpose, meaning and hope within the provenance of its Creator. That, presumably, was the Gospel which was Jesus of Nazareth: the how-and-when of the Resurrection are nowhere near so important as the understanding that, when 'God raised him up and declared him to be Lord and Christ', God was saying 'Yes' to his world.

> MINISTRY is the proclamation of God's 'Yes' to the world by *whoever* proclaims it, by *whoever* demands a reaction to it, in *whatever* field it is proclaimed. And that proclamation is laid on *every* Christian at baptism. . . 'This is our Faith. . .'

This is the bit that got lost between the rhinoceros's horn and his rear. The sort of new words we need for talking about ourselves (since the other words have got themselves tangled with all sorts of nuances) is, therefore, something like 'Evangelistic Confraternity' –

– where 'Evangelistic' carries no context of churchmanship but refers equally to the chap who feels he ought to push tracts through doors and the woman who feels she ought to get involved in politics wherever they do these things, because both these people feel that, this way, they can proclaim to the World its purpose, meaning and hope within the provenance of its Creator. . .

– and where 'Confraternity' makes the Church once again a phenomenon at which the world-outside-the-church may stare and exclaim, 'These Christians! How they love one another!' and, one may hope, 'How they love the world!'

***

Parables and parallels must not be pushed too far, so we must leave our Zoo and have a look at ourselves.

One of the language-failures from which we started has meant that, in order to talk about the bits, we have separated 'Worship' and 'Mission/Ministry' in our thinking. (How often does one find church council sub-committees, one called the 'Worship Committee' and another called the 'Mission Committee'. And how often is 'Mission' something 'they' do and we 'support'. It is so much easier to run far off and burn incense than to light a candle at home.)

One contention of this essay is that ministry and worship are inseparable – indeed, that we separate them in our thinking at our peril.

Before we go on, then, let us have a brief self-examination of what we consider to be appropriate actions and involvements in worship/ministry for the non-ordained members of the Evangelistic Confraternity.

Over the next two pages there are 'Pools Coupons' for you to fill in. The frame works through the sort of hierarchical progression which seems to be commonly assumed among congregations. Have a quiet think, and tick the boxes which you approve:

M = Male, F = Female.

All = Something that could be done by all members of the congregation.

Some = Something done by 'selected' members of the congregation.

Theol. Obj. – Tick this if you feel there are scriptural (or other theological) grounds why the non-ordained should not do this.

Un. Prej. – This will take some honesty! Unreasoning Prejudice. . . and we all have it. It includes saying, 'But we have never done anything like that here!'

Afterwards, you might care to get together with a few of your fellow-punters to discuss the variations on your coupons, rationally, of course. No 'overcoming by indignation', or holier-than-thou.

Other questions that occur:

(1) Is there a connection between the two Coupons
  (a) for you?
  (b) for the non-churchgoer?

(2) As you go down the lists, does the Parish Priest's job gradually disappear – a sort of Cheshire Cat grin?

(3) Would you want to make changes in the order of progression suggested by the order of items in the lists? Any others you would want to add?

THE JOB OF THE LAITY *INSIDE* CHURCH IS. . .

	M	F	All	Some	Theol. Obj.	Un. Obj.
Read Lessons						
Choose the hymns for Sunday						
Lead a discussion group						
Lead a Bible Study						
Lead the prayers at Matins or Evensong						
Lead Intercessions at the Communion Service						
Read the Gospel at Communion						
Take Matins/Evensong (NOT preach)						
Take Matins/Evensong and choose a 'third lesson other than from Bible.'						
Prepare a sermon (Subject to Vicar's vetting)						
Take a part in the Baptism service						
Take a part in the Marriage service						
Take a part in the Funeral service						
Lead Eucharistic Worship apart from Absolution/Thanksgiving/ Blessing						
Preside at the Eucharist – given sanction of PCC and the Bishop						

THE JOB OF THE LAITY *OUTSIDE* THE CHURCH IS. . .

	M	F	All	Some	Theol. Obj.	Un. Obj.
Assist with fund-raising						
Assist with Sunday School/Youth Club						
Act as street/district Warden – 'Vicar's eye and ear'						
Magazine distributor						
Act as welcomer of newcomers						
Act as Home/Sick visitor						
Act as Visitor/Evangelist						
Assist as Hospital Visitor						
Staff Office in Vicar's absence						
Assist in Baptism interviews						
Assist in Marriage interviews						
Assist in Confirmation preparation						
Follow up bereavement						
Initial contact for Baptisms						
Initial contact for Marriage preparation						
Initial contact in bereavement						
Visitor in counselling situation						

FOUR

The Evangelistic Fraternity I

You probably found that the ticks in our Pools Coupon got thinner as you went downwards, and the reason was probably either your own shyness or a feeling that some of the tasks mentioned needed a specific bit of training which you do not have. It would probably surprise you to know that, hitherto, few of the clergy have had any specific training for the tasks mentioned – tasks which many would feel to be the parson's job. A moment's thought on each of them (apart from the Sacramental roles. . . for the moment) will surely say that these are not 'parson's job', but very much 'Christian's duty'.

Where, then, has the thinking got hooked up?

Almost certainly in the way we think of ordained ministers, and especially in the way we tend to think automatically and primarily of the full-time, stipendiary, ordained ministry. The chap earns his living by it, so it must be his job.

Not so. We, the Church, ordained him because we exist **to tell ourselves a story** – the story of what God did with Jesus of Nazareth – because we believe that story indicates God's purpose for his world. So we exist, too, to tell that story to the world: a story of the love, the forgiveness, the care, the sharing-in-the-world, the constant creating, the purpose of uniting all things 'in Christ' which has been revealed to us as – 'This is what God is like'. . . the story of unquenchable hope.

Even the elephants get quite trumpety about it!

Professor Moltmann, for instance, in *Theology and Joy* (SCM Press, 1973): '. . .the centre of (Christian) theology is the liberating game of resurrection-faith.' And even that is not a new idea except in the way Moltmann expressed it. As early as the 4th century, the Cappodocian Fathers talked about the Dance (perichoresis) of the Trinity and, in Christ and through the Spirit, Creation was caught up in the Dance. . . hence your hymn, 'Lord of the Dance'.

So MOST of our worship ought to look a bit like the illustration below. . .

It's the first thing we have to say about God, for it is about our being *claimed* by God in Baptism, *sent out* by God in Confirmation, *redeemed* by Christ and *sustained* by God in Communion. . . and all of it a rejoicing in the hope that is set before us.

So does your Worship look like that?

It is so important to us, this story, that we have enshrined certain parts of it in people. We have set aside some to whom we have said:

> You alone shall speak the words of Forgiveness. You alone shall repeat the words of the Great Thanksgiving which enshrines the memory of what Christ did for us in 'the night that he was betrayed'. You alone shall pronounce that Blessing which God pronounced on the World when He raised Christ up. These things are so important to us that we embody them in you. . . not because you are more worthy than anyone else, but because we, the Church, make you a SYMBOL FIGURE – a Priest – so that we may remind ourselves over and over again that WE are a Living Temple where the Father is to be worshipped in all places and at all times by lives laid down for the World as Christ laid down his own life – that God might raise our lives in union with Christ.

That is what you meant when you Ordained Fred and Joe at the hands of the Bishop, whom you, the Church, appointed as yet another enshrined truth about yourselves: that you are called to be shepherds to the world around you. This is such a high calling, so close to the whole purpose of Christ, that we shall regard our bishops as the symbol of what is to come – that unity when 'Christ shall be all and in you all'. A central SYMBOL FIGURE then.

And, to remind ourselves of how our shepherding is to be carried out, we made one other symbol – a servant. A deacon. A foot-washer, because that foot-washing of Maundy

Thursday is to govern every aspect of our approach to one another and to the world.

No, you did not ordain them to a job. You ordained them as SYMBOL PEOPLE.

And then you did a very naughty thing!

You took your SYMBOL MINISTERS and made them SUBSTITUTE MINISTERS. . . so that you could duck out of the awkward bits of YOUR MINISTRY. They were the chaps who obviously ought to stand in for you with the awkwards biddies and the cussed squad. Someone you could blame when you, the Church, failed to do the caring and cuddling and straight-talking and dirty-feet washing and grubby-hand holding. . . your ministry. . . because you are the Church. Your ordained folk you put there just to remind you. They are the Church too, but ministry belongs to the whole Evangelistic Fraternity. It is not just the Elephants who trumpet: it's all of us. In fact, the word 'evangelist' means 'someone who heralds (trumpets) the arrival of his Lord', and we are all in that job, for Christ's sake. An ordained man should be a minister among the ministers, a fellow amongst the fellows in the Evangelistic Confraternity, a gospeller with the gospellers.

There have been endless, wasteful attempts to find a job-specification for him. Again, this was largely issue-ducking, for there is, scripturally speaking, only a very limited area in which to look, and which your search will eventually be unable to avoid : the more specific gifts of ministry all have their definition within Ephesians, 4:12. They exist 'to equip God's people for work in his service, to building up the body of Christ'. In the older version (which is, in this case, verbally more accurate for our purposes), it reads: '. . .building up the faithful for the work of ministry'. That leaves no doubt as to who are the ministers! You who are baptized.

In the Elephant's words:

> There needs always to be a living voice to interpret the Scripture and continue the witness. This witness must be given by others besides the ordained ministers; but it is they who are responsible for knowing what the Christian teaching is, and seeing that it is expounded (Gabriel Hebert again).

Harvey goes a little further. Describing the many facets of the life of a Christian community, from worship to administration, from education to the relief of need, he says: 'Clearly no minister could cope with these personally. . . He is first and foremost, a 'minister of Word and Sacraments. But his responsibility will not end with these. If any of the tasks fails to be carried out, it is he and he alone who will be ultimately responsible.' Harvey quotes from the earliest known ordination rite (in the *Apostolic Tradition* – i.e. 3rd century):

> . . .the words. . . which specify the task to which the presbyter is ordained: 'Look upon this thy servant and impart to him the spirit of grace and counsel, that he may. . . govern thy people in a pure heart.' Nothing is said here of liturgical functions. The prayer simply implores the gifts of the Spirit for the kind of general leadership and authority. . . the one distinctive task of the presbyterate in the early centuries.

And, of course, we must not forget Professor Macquarrie's 'principles' for the organisation of the congregation, 'collegiality, con-celebration and, not least co-theologising'. The ordained man is to be the 'theologiser-with' the People of God, not the 'theologiser-for'.

But if he has become 'theologiser-for', that may well be your fault, my reader!

So would you like to stop for a minute and chat with someone about what this word 'theology' means for you. Are the Creeds enough? Can one, Christianly, theologise about things unmentioned in the Bible – atom bombs, say? Does the Bible have the last word? Always? Should we consider the God-insights of other religions? If 'the world sets the agenda' is there any way in which the world also dictates the theology?

FIVE

The Evangelistic Fraternity II

Leadership, Authority (where that represents reference back to the total awareness of the whole Body of Christ, past and present), Responsibility, Co-theologising – these will always be ultimate tasks which the Evangelistic Confraternity lays on its ordained ministers over and above their sacramental role. They are that by which the Confraternity focusses its being and its purpose. But they are also part of the Confraternity, not its sole arm. The muscle-stuff is for all who call themselves Christ's, and none may abdicate the calling to ministry, since the supreme picture of the Confraternity is found in 'doing what Jesus did in the night that he was betrayed' – 'laying down life' for the world.

So the world, which God loved that much, is the object of ministry, not the mere purity of our own detergent-white souls. They, it seems, will only achieve not only whiteness but brightness as we risk getting them dirty for the others.

How to minister, then? There will be as many answers to that as there are Christians. For some, singing hymns on street corners may seem to be their demanded response for the moment; others may feel the need to 'baptize' their jobs; some will feel bound to seek ordination; others will know no peace until they identify themselves with the world's area of intense poverty. Definition is not possible, because God is an extravagant Creator of endless variety and made the shape of your nose and the colour of your hair unique for his own purposes. The Church is most truly the Evangelistic Fellowship when it is using to the full that immense variety of its hair and its noses.

Oh! Those unique gifts, all God-intended, and we have let them get institutionally flattened and brylcreemed!

But never get cynical about it. The Christian Church has always been filled, and still is, by those who are first among those who concern themselves for their neighbours' well-being, who weep with those that weep and rejoice with those who are rejoicing. Praise be! Your ministry is going on all the while. The big question, though, is how does that get identified by those to whom you minister as the ministry of the Evangelistic Confraternity, the ministry for Christ's sake and in Christ's name? Most of us, one may suspect, would be very coy about telling our fellows that.

And, even if you take the first and immediate ring of your ministry – this thing called a parish – are you sure you cover everyone in it? For most of us it is a sadly humbling exercise to look through the Register of Electors and ask, 'Who weeps with him or rejoices with her when they need someone?'

And what do they really want on those occasions?

Unquestionably, unchurched though the majority of the population may be, it would still instinctively want to say 'the Church'. Doubtless, most mean by that 'the Vicar', but that possibility has been unreal since the beginning of the twentieth century – and probably long before : unreal, in fact, since the growth of the population, and its movement, made nonsense of the mediaeval definition of parish boundaries. The idea of one or two men 'ministering' to five or ten thousand people reduces 'ministry' to ministry-to-the-chosen-few or 'total ministry' is having time to say, 'Hallo, how are you?' and hoping that nobody tells you – because it will mean missing out another hundred 'Hallos'.

It is time to face that roundly. Even if you have an Electoral Roll of 600 (not too many in that state, one may think) in a parish of 8,000, the Church cannot be effectively 'ministering' to the other 7,400 if that ministry is left to vicar and curate. Not even if you add three non-stipendiary ministers.

In brief, we have reached a stage where the deployment of all the hair-styles and noses has become crucial. . . *and we have therefore reached a stage where a new addition to Representative Ministry must be made: an addition which may commend the Ministry of the whole Evangelistic Fellowship to, and for the sake of, those outside the Church. . . for this God-beloved World.*

It is that Representative Ministry which is currently being called the 'Lay Pastorate'. How then shall that pastorate be commended to that world to which it is primarily to minister?

Here we seem to have three arrows to our bow.

The first is that symbol-figure of all ministry, the bishop. If the parish or the parish priest 'goes it alone', then all will be shipwreck. The world outside will see it as no more than a gimmick which is something to do with St. Leger's Church and nothing to do with them. So then, perhaps it is something that the Archdeacon or the Rural Dean can do? With all apology to our worthy Arch-d's and R Ds, the world outside has not the foggiest clue what they are. But Fred and Flo, Tracey and Kevin, do know what the bishop is. He's the managing director, and what he says goes. In that case (in the spirit of the opening verse of 2 Corinthians 6), regardless of what we think, it is the bishop who must be seen to be instituting a pastorate scheme and authorising the pastors; for ministry is two-sided: the ministered-to must accept ministry, and the quickest route to that is, by definition, the best. That route is unquestionably the Bishop.

Arrow two is an unexpected one. Although Fred and Flo, Tracey and Kevin never come near the church, it somehow gets around that there are those who take a leading part in the church's worship: 'Them as does things up front on Sundays'. Because of that, they have some sort of esteem in the eyes of the world. We may see it differently, but what we see does not matter. The world definitely sets the agenda here. Readers, for instance, are marked people whether they like it or not. (Another happy memory: being told, of one departed worthy: 'He was a very important man in the church. Used to shake hands with everyone at the door on Sundays.') All right, it's daft! But if it is there, let's use it.

Arrow three. The local church is always good copy for the local press and local radio, so use that too. The beginning of a Lay Pastorate has to be a well-planned publicity campaign; not for publicity's sake, but so that the pastors are marked in the world's eyes as those who speak in the name of the whole Church, those to whom one may turn to find a needed hand or word or prayer. 'Exposure' is the media-word, and such exposure makes one vulnerable; but it may be regarded as a sure maxim 'No vulnerability, no ministry'.

Another point at which to stop for stock-taking. . .

How do you see the Bishop? Chief Minister/Chief Administrator?

In your own parishes, how do you exploit the possibilities of purely human contact presented by such obvious things as Baptisms and Marriages? (you – not the Vicar)

Do you ever have any events (a simple coffee-evening, say) just to welcome folk to the community when they move in (never mind whether they are churchgoers or Buddhists), or would you think the Church has no responsibility in that direction?

SIX

Getting Down To It

From this point onward, the reader must forgive me if I move into first persons, singular or plural, for this is a description of how I and We worked it out in one group of parishes. Some of its content I would reckon to be fundamentally necessary to any situation. But that is only what I think. What is more important is that, for every parish or group there is one first and great commandment which you shall write upon the posts of your doors and hang above your beds. . .

. . .because the Lord your God made you you, and them them, and you must comb your own hair and follow your own noses.

What is important and in common, is that your pastors are called to their pastorate by the congregation whose Ministry they are to spearhead. There are no volunteers. We went about it like this:

(1) We talked through the sort of thing you have been reading at our Annual Parochial Church Meeting.

(2) We discussed it further with the new PCC, and then I asked them to think of folk within the congregation of whom they would say, 'This is the person I think of when I ask myself, 'What is a Christian really like?' '

There are always some in every church, no matter how small the congregation. The Spirit has willed it so. . . old, young, male, female. You know them. And you can trust the Spirit to direct your course.

(3) We agreed on a three-month silence, to be concluded at a Parish Communion at which each member of the PCC would write down those names which had come uppermost in the thinking. There were to be no decisions, however charitable, on the basis of 'It would be good for her', or 'It would be something for him to do'. These were to be ministers among the ministers.

The unanimity of naming was a source of surprise.

I saw each one individually and put it to them on the basis that the Church had named them, and they had to give me very good reason why not. Whether they wanted to take on the Lay Pastorate was totally irrelevant. One of those named gave good business and family reasons why the Pastorate was not for him at that time. The other five all accepted the damand on them – one man, four women whose ages ranged from the sixties to the twenties. So to business, and as soon as you mention that within the

"Of course, if you were to spend a couple of years doing the Bishop's certificate, you *might* do some useful work for the Church. . ."

C of E, with its sadly good tradition of academia, the cry goes up, 'What training are you going to give them?' and Bright Spark One wants 'Pastoral' Training (if we only knew what that was), BS2 wants to 'ground 'em in theology', BS3 is sure they cannot manage without a course on counselling, and you have a ready-made four-year course for the B P (Bachelor of Pastoralia). . . which may have some connection with spirit, but stops anybody moving anywhere.

One must recognise the cry for what it is: one of fear. And understandably so. The laity (in humility?) are quite sure that there are special skills and special knowledge involved. Indeed, many of them will hope so because that rationalises 'why not'. . . much too busy you know, what with work and the kids. . . might do it when I retire. . .

Now a Lay Pastorate whose average age is over 60 might well be a collection of saints, but it would hardly be representative. The cry comes from the clergy too. Interestingly, talking to clergy about Lay Pastorate immediately seems to produce talk about 'job-specification' and 'role', and, very often, a 'professionalised' recital of the 'mysteries' of pastoral work. The defence mechanism is, therefore, to see oneself as a 'trainer' if one cannot stop this tide.

(I would argue that this indeed is the future role of the clergy, but not in this withdrawing sense of producing courses.)

***

We decided, therefore, that Initial Training was to be a basic examination of the 'tools of the trade' – scripturally, I suppose, 'looking to the nets'. An immediate danger presented itself: any sort of training, even if it were only initial training, presented the temptation for Lay Pastors and the rest of the Evangelistic Confraternity alike to ascribe to it expertise. This would all too easily lead to the L Ps becoming a new substitute ministry and, if that happened, we would merely have created a new complication.

It was evident, therefore, that there was a Second Great Commandment – very like the first – namely, this:

. . .a text to be kept above beds, on door-posts, between the eyes. . .

But while we are on Two we might as well go the whole hog and have Ten. . .

Ten Commandments for the Lay Pastorate

1. The Lay Pastor must minister both to the Church in the leadership of worship and to the world as a spearhead of the Evangelistic Confraternity.
2. The LP must share with the clergy in the whole pastoral gamut, not solely in a personally selected area.
3. The LP must be designated by the local congregation – neither volunteer nor merely nominee of the parish clergy.
4. The LP must be given room to develop individual gifts.
5. The LP must be identified to the area (parish/group/ whatever) as ministering in the name of the whole local Evangelistic Confraternity. . . not just 'another do-gooder' in the world's eyes.
6. The local Christians must not be allowed to relapse into yet another (albeit different) substitute ministry.
7. Age or sex of LP is irrelevant.
8. Theological expertise is not a criterion. Theology is, presumably, the interpretation of experience in the context of 'The All', tested by Christians by reference to Christ. Theologising is, therefore, 'way of life' rather than 'exercise' or 'qualification'.
9. Preaching is not an objective – it belongs more logically to the Reader (though reader is an illogical enough title these days). For purposes of taking services, why not a third (extra-biblical) lesson instead of a sermon?. . .most of the best stuff is already in books anyway.
10. Action by Lay Pastors and Clergy alike should always be referred back to the whole representative ministry team. (Proviso: of course confidentiality is confidentiality. That applies to the whole Evangelistic Confraternity – a word that must never be broken. Even if wider advice is felt to be needful it must never by sought without prior permission of the one ministered to.)

This seems to be a logical break-point to discuss things so far, for the 'Commandments' represent a summary of the preceding thoughts. Take each one to bits.

Are we in danger of multiplying ministries? Is that necessarily dangerous? Any ideas on how to avoid the tendency towards a new substitute ministry? Any more 'commandments' you would want to add? (But don't end up with a new Leviticus, will you.)

Five Ways to stop this ministry stuff
"WE CAN MANAGE...."
"I WOULDN'T IF I WERE YOU..."
"WE NEVER HAVE"
"IT WILL EMPTY THE CHURCH"
"THEY'LL NEVER ACCEPT IT"

SEVEN

Tools of the Trade

The Initiation Training of the Lay Pastors finally took the shape of ten sessions before their actual commissioning by the Bishop. These sessions sat on a fairly loose skeleton, for the Lay Pastors were thrown immediately into taking various parts in various services, and such things as leading intercessions, pace, timing, enunciation – all produced their own discussion and bits of practice. The aim was to wean them so that, by the time they were commissioned, they would be over that initial terror which comes even from reading a lesson!

The subject of the first session may seem surprising. . .

Walk into Church. . .

It is the first contact with it for someone – and because of that, move heaven and earth to keep the building available, even if it means replacing all the brass and silver with wood to satisfy the insurers. So who locks and unlocks it night and morning?

What hits you as you come through the door?

- Scrappy notice-board? Out-of-date notices?
- Books all over the place? (Choir worst offenders?)
- Altar(s) uncovered and uncared for? Untrimmed candles, wax everywhere? (Bats not receiving proper attention?!) 'Fair white linen' cloths thrown at it? Ornaments not tidy?

- Chairs all over the place? And hassocks?
- Fallen or dead flowers? Flower-arrangers have a conspiracy to leave little plastic watering-cans and vicious secateurs on altar-rails, credence tables, window-sills. . . just give 'em a flat surface and see! As for the green stuff they push flowers into. . .
- Remember that stale hymn-boards smell like yesterday's kippers.

Take trouble over arrangements for things like cleaning-rotas, flower-arrangement, sidesmen (including 'hosts' for occasional services) – these are not just 'the mechanicals': they are 'doing their thing' God-wards. How do you tell them that?

- Be fussy. (and happy if you are told you are too fussy). If 'my house shall be called a house of prayer', will it look that way when a stranger comes in? Will it make him want to be still even though he has come initially out of curiosity?

An empty church should say that it is ready for the next act of worship, not, 'Thank God that's over! Let's get home.'

A building reflects the thought of those who use it. . . and your building is the first tool of your gospelling for someone who walks in. When, you do not know. You are required to have the lamps trimmed.

***

The full text of the end hand-out of our first training session has been included here because it represents the general route of our initial training. The poor old local congregation now looks as though it is hauling enough luggage around to make the 'burden' of Bunyan's 'Christian' look like a lunch-pack. With building slung albatross-like round its neck, with a whole weight of ecclesiastical administration, with an attempt to provide for what too often look like state-substitute services – how can 'the church' ever move?

That is what it feels like. But it is a delusion: a trick played on us by institutionalism.

The move to full-size ministry starts with a change of attitude: a stock-taking of what we already have in order to explore its possibilities if we get it in its proper order of priority. The building is an obvious place to start. Once call it 'the House of God', and you have put it (piously, no doubt) at the top of the pile – and posed yourself some theological problems on 'the God who is everywhere present' into the bargain. Make it what it is – the visual aid we have inherited, the coming-together-place of the Evangelistic Confraternity, the place of 'doing what Jesus did in the night he was betrayed' for this place, this village, this town, this suburb. Now we can play with it, draw with it, use it for what it is: a tool for ministry.

***

Session II (which extended into 'three' as well), we called *Prepare to meet thy God*. It dealt with routine considerations of looking after the congregation, preparing well ahead for festivals (most of the Church thinks they just happen), planning the involvement of others in acts of worship, choosing hymns well ahead. And that led us to a fairly thorough consideration of all those tool-books we have around the place, to our own personal devotional practice as strengthening for service, and to the mental and practical Saturday-preparation-for-Sunday.

All very inward-looking so far, you might think! But loaded, of course. . . for we come to *Session III* (by this time 4½!):

We started digging around the vestry into Registers, Banns Forms, Baptism Forms. Practical issues first: the Occasional Services, how to prepare for them, the bits of paper associated with them. . . and we were there! How can we use these paper tools for ministry? You don't have to sit there like a clerk on the other side of the desk. You can call on folk with the Banns or Baptism things – or invite them round for a cuppa. . . perhaps a few couples or Mums and Dads together. That's reconciliation: joining people together and leaving to find this warm God of ours in one another in the shared great experiences and moments.

By this time the potential Lay Pastors were being sent round to various houses with these particular bits of paper as occasion arose. This not only served as a 'baptism'; it brought also from them the observation that it was easy to call on folk one did not know too well if you had a specific 'thing' for them. This led us to the exploration of possible 'things' – taking over an occasional magazine round, and door-knocking instead of letter-box-popping; baptism-anniversary-card deliveries. We even invented more paper: a 'fill-in' visiting card which we had printed (after some decent designing) which simply said, '. . .from all of us in the Windcross parishes' and could be filled in with a suitable note of condolence, congratulation or shared rejoicing according to the occasion. We added to that a note about the Thanksgiving for the Birth of a Child which invited some serious thought about Baptism, and another note about Churchyard Memorials which would make an occasion for a post-bereavement visit. One can almost invent them at will, and if they ease the path into confidence, so be it: any tool of pastoral contact is, *per se*, good.

Surprisingly (and interestingly to the social psychologist) the easiest approach for the budding LPs proved to be the simple call of welcome to those who had newly moved in. Not surprisingly, the hospital call provoked the most discussion. Perhaps because we are a long way from the hospitals that serve us, this particular visit is always welcomed – the sense of belonging once again. For the first time the LPs began to experience the *persona* sense, where one is welcomed because of what one represents – Community.

It is at this point that one has to face the issue of what being Evangelistic means. Should one go scratching around to create opportunities to preach the Word? Should one officiously attempt to turn the situation into verbal prayer? Should one offer the particular rites of the Church that apply to this situation. I personally think not. Of course, one must listen for any hint of desire in these directions, and one must be prepared to meet them – even in the sudden request that will come from the most unexpected person, 'Will you say a prayer with me?' But, for me, the essence of the Pastoral Evangelist is 'to *be* for this other, this beloved', not to lead him or her in some direction that would merely satisfy one's own sense of achievement. The pastoral ear is a hundred times more important than the pastoral mouth, and one must not presume to trespass on the Spirit's domain.

But there you may wish to argue. . .

The last of the Initial Training sessions contained two elements:

- a listing of common knowledge on addresses and phone numbers of social agencies from DHSS and Social Services, through agencies such as the Citizens Advice Bureau, Local Housing Authority, various Support Groups, and so on.
- practice in administration of the Chalice.

The binding together of these two things served to emphasise the inseparability of Worship and Mission.

EIGHT

Getting Off the Ground

Meanwhile, back at the works end. . .

The Initial Training had all been timed after discussion with the Bishop on –

- what scope he was prepared to give to the Lay Pastorate in church
- when he would be available to commission the LPs.

The second of these presents no problems. The first is a matter for very careful thought, by the PCC as much as by the Bishop. Are the pastors to assist in the administration of Communion? What part/s of the Communion Service may they take? What services may they take alone? What part may they take in Baptisms, Marriages and Funeral Services? These things are an extremely important first step, since any retraction after commissioning will appear to the outside world as a lack of confidence in the scheme, and to the Lay Pastors as a lack of confidence in them. So this is serious business, not just another irrelevant chat on the PCC agenda. And, incidentally, it is also an opportunity for the parish to recognise the Bishop as Chief Pastor rather than merely The Boss.

So, too, concurrently with the Initial Training came the publicity build-up.

The Parish Magazine obviously carried fairly detailed reports on what was happening. The local press was informed about two months before the Commissioning, and the local radio station about one month. A complete house-to-house circulation of the parish used leaflets ostensibly inviting everyone to the Commissioning. One could be fairly sure they would not all come, but the important thing about it was that the Lay Pastors' names figured prominently. A fortnight before the service, specific invitations were sent to the leaders of local groups, political and social: the WI, the Parish Council, the Brownie leader, and so on. In short, anything to get those outside the Church to realise that these Lay Pastors were going to be available to them.

The commissioning itself had been arranged to coincide with a confirmation. Not always possible, of course, but certainly much to be desired since it serves to point the togetherness of these two elements of the Christian's life, both for the Lay Pastors and for the whole Evangelistic Confraternity.

The commissioning itself must be simple and direct involving:

(a) A declaration of the wish and will of the Incumbent and PCC to use these persons as a spearhead of the pastoral work in the parish.

(b) A declaration of the will of the congregation to accept the pastoral leadership of the LPs and to share fully in that work.

(c) A statement of the areas of ministry in which the Bishop is prepared to give the LPs authority.

(d) A statement that the office of Lay Pastor is to last for a period of three years and may, within that time, be terminated by the Bishop.

This last may need some explanation. It was felt necessary to indicate clearly that the Lay Pastor's office was localised to the parish, and that there was to be no chance of the congregation coming to think of them as permanent substitutes for their own task. The retention of the authority of the Bishop over the whole is necessary, not only to highlight his own sacramental role, but also to guard against embarrassment for any future incumbent who might move into the parish with no particular sympathy for a Lay Pastorate scheme.

***

It is at this point that the incumbent has to say his prayers and bite his nails! There is no shallow end to this pool.

> This is no place to record personal agonies, but I resolved to do no pastoral visiting for two months, save in bereavement, unless the Lay Pastors told me whom I should visit.

Surprisingly, the heavens did not fall. . . but God is very lax about telling you they are not going to. Instead, the Lay Pastors kept coming back to me with the difficulties of Mr. X or the loneliness of old Mrs. Y, and fortnightly (for this time) we had a get-together to discuss what had been said and done, and a heart-search session about its rightness and adequacy. Suffice it to say that it worked. The acceptance of the Lay Pastors, especially from those fuzzy edges of the Church, was much wider and more welcoming than we had ever dared to hope.

From there on we met monthly (as we have done ever since), arranging services, thinking ahead, talking through various individual and corporate needs in the parish, deciding who should make the first call on those newly moved in, and so on. . . the sort of stuff that makes up any ministerial staff meeting. It was the equivalent (save for the preaching ministry) of having five curates in the parish.

Of course there were some within the parish who objected. That was easily dealt with by asking those who were not prepared to accept Lay Ministry to say so. These are then the vicar's pastoral ministry – with no attempt at forcing the issue. It is no more than happens to a new incumbent who has to wait until God, time or chance throws the pastoral opportunity into the lap. After two years, the number of objectors had reduced to little more than a handful.

The first year of the Lay Pastorate must needs be a settling one, for the sake of the parish as much as the pastors, with all the LPs tackling all the range of normal parish pastoralia. The 'accidents' of normal routine will quickly bring about those opportunities which produce acceptance: in our own case, for example, I was taken ill on Easter Eve – the Parish Priest's nightmare! The Lay Pastors moved in and took Matins – and everybody was so surprised, they avowed it was the best Easter they had had. . . the absence of the vicar may have been a contributory factor! Then, while I was on holiday, a child died; the immediate response of a Lay pastor assured everyone of the fact that this was not merely 'second-best' ministry.

Year two brought new questions from pastors and PCCs alike. The LPs began to feel the need to be part of the administration of Communion to those unable to get to church. They accompanied me on several occasions, and then the bishop allowed them to take the Reserved Sacrament our on their own, with the result that we were able, at major feasts, to send them straight from the altar so that our sick ones were receiving the Sacrament on the same occasion as we were.

The PCC then started to ask the 64-thousand-dollar question: Why, if the priest is a symbol-figure of the sacramental life of the whole Evangelistic Confraternity in this place, was it possible that the Confraternity should be without its identifying sacramental symbol (the Eucharist) simply because no priest was available when the vicar was on holiday? The immediate contra to this was to say that communicants should then go to another church. The PCC replied that, while they were always happy to go to another church for particular occasions and specific identity situations, they felt that the Sunday Eucharist was (a) a particularly local family thing and that (b) a particular focussing of their ministry (hats in the air for 'their'!) in this place, with these people at this time. The upshot of long debate was that the bishop allowed the parish to receive Communion from the Reserved Sacrament, the LPs taking the whole service save for an 'us' Absolution, omitting the Thanksgiving, and concluding with a corporate saying of the Grace.

I mention all this simply to show the extent to which the advent of the Lay Pastorate stretches the theologising of the whole Confraternity.

The outside triumph was reached when, in my absence, a Lay Pastor dealt with a bereavement and brought in a neighbouring priest to take the funeral service. The comment which met me when I visited the family on my return was that Mr. So-and-so had taken the service very beautifully, but they would have preferred to have Mrs. — (one of the Lay Pastors) taking the service 'because we know her'. Is it too much to hope that they had somehow got an inkling in the saddest of circumstances, is not a little to do with relationship?

The Lay Pastors themselves started, at this stage, to develop some of their own things. One became involved in doing the Bishop's Certificate and ended up as an instructor on the Diocesan Course. Another pursued a more intense activity within the work of the Parish Council. A third, who was having her first child, naturally gathered around her other expectant mums and produced a co-operation amongst them which solved all sorts of baby-sitting problems. . . and, in the meantime, carried on administering the Sacrament until the week before her child was born. The experience of administering-with or being-administered-to by a young woman large with life was, I think, unforgettable for all of us. I confess I had to spend a long kneel before the altar to de-mist my eyes before I could end the service: Bethlehem rather jumped on the place, and incarnation became very much a part of Incarnation.

The most intense thought that emerged was the concern for Community. It expressed itself in the gathering-in (to community, not church) of those moving into the area: introductory coffee-evenings; invitations to meet others with similar interests; the production of a list of all the activities, sacred and secular, which went on in the area, along with names of organisers – clearly there are endless opportunities here that matter. Most importantly, it was a concern that affected the attitudes of the whole congregation.

Then, along with a preparation for Lent, came the formation of house groups. While the LPs were entirely responsible for setting them up, not one group was led by a pastor. They coaxed or tricked all sorts of people into abilities they did not know they had – but mostly coaxed. The culmination of this came with my being asked to preach an Advent Course of three sermons with written copies for subsequent discussion.

In short, we have reached the situation envisaged by Macquarrie where we see ourselves as collegiate. What a terrible indictment of the Laos of God that a term such as 'clerical loneliness' should have crept into the vocabulary of the Church! We have come as near to con-celebration as the present situation will allow, and we co-theologise at all sorts of levels.

The question that will naturally arise is: 'Have you lost nobody on the way?' Here we are lucky. One of the advantages of being a group of churches is that one of them can always be kept as 'The Ark' – a place for those who are unwilling to face any necessity for change. There our handful live out their Christian life quite happily ministered-to. The geographical parish itself is tended in exactly the same way as the others; but it is surely significant that there are more folk from that parish who worship regularly in another church in the group than go to the church in that parish. Nevertheless, it must obviously be a matter of some tender concern that one should either use the buildings or use the time-table to allow for those who find change difficult to face, no matter how necessary it is.

At this point, you might like to have a second look at the Football Coupons to see whether any of your positions have changed or are changing.

Conclusion

The latter pages of this essay have been a skeletal resumé of what has happened in one group of parishes. They sit under the dictum of our 'first and great commandment for parishes' simply because, if we are really examining our mission, we shall never be able to predict 'where the wind comes from or where it is blowing'. Like the Rum-Tum-Tugger, the Spirit 'will do what he do do, and there's no doing anything about it'.

I could add the experience of a former parish where the Lay Pastors carried through a long sequestration during which the numbers of the congregation increased. (The obvious comment will be treated with contempt.) They continued to lead that parish while the new incumbent added another to the cure and took over as Rural Dean.

No doubt, those who have given their lay ministry full play would all tell a different tale. The important thing is that the adventure has to be tried, for we are faced with a decision about whether we believe God is a God of history or not. The decline during this century of the full-time, paid manpower needed to maintain the institutional Church of England as it has been conceived during the previous four centuries demands an either/or: either this is a nasty accident, or it is the will of a God who is demanding something new. There are no other choices.

The Tiller Report was significant in that it represented the first full-scale attempt to answer the question: 'What sort of institution ought we to be considering?' where 'institution' equals whatever organisation might be considered most effective for the Evangelistic activity of the Confraternity. But Canon Tiller's concept, and any other that may emerge, will undoubtedly depend on the deployment of the whole Confraternity, not just on the deployment of its ordained men. Their deployment and their training must necessarily depend on whatever overall model is to be realised.

The decisions about lay ministry are the foundation stones of any Church for the twentieth century.

Meanwhile, merely to look back in nostalgia will have the same effect on us as on Lot's wife.